FOOTBALL LEGENDS

Troy Aikman

Terry Bradshaw

John Elway

Brett Favre

Michael Irvin

Vince Lombardi

John Madden

Dan Marino

Joe Montana

Walter Payton

Jerry Rice

Barry Sanders

Deion Sanders

Emmitt Smith

Lawrence Taylor

Steve Young

CHELSEA HOUSE PUBLISHERS

WALTER PAYTON

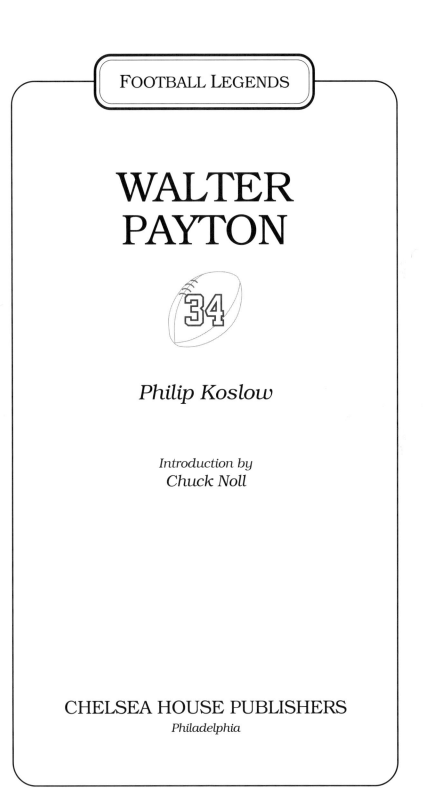

Philip Koslow

Introduction by
Chuck Noll

CHELSEA HOUSE PUBLISHERS
Philadelphia

Produced by Daniel Bial and Associates
New York, New York.

Picture research by Alan Gottlieb
Cover illustration by Bradford Brown

5 7 9 8 6

Koslow, Philip.
    Walter Payton / Philip Koslow.
      p.   cm. — (Football legends)
    Includes bibliographical references (p.) and index.
    ISBN 0-7910-2455-5
    1. Payton, Walter, 1954– —Juvenile literature. 2. Football
players—United States—Biography—Juvenile literature. 3. National
Football League—Juvenile literature. [1. Payton, Walter, 1954– . 2.
Football players. 3. Afro-Americans—Biography.] I. Title.
II. Series.
GV939.P39K87 1994
796.332'092—dc20
    [B]   94-1352
                                                             CIP
                                                              AC

CONTENTS

A WINNING ATTITUDE

Chuck Noll

Don't ever fall into the trap of believing, "I could never do that. And I won't even try—I don't want to embarrass myself." After all, most top athletes had no idea what they could accomplish when they were young. A secret to the success of every star quarterback and sure-handed receiver is that they tried. If they had not tried, if they had not persevered, they would never have discovered how far they could go and how much they could achieve.

You can learn about trying hard and overcoming challenges by being a sports fan. Or you can take part in organized sports at any level, in any capacity. The student messenger at my high school is now president of a university. A reserve ballplayer who got very little playing time in high school now owns a very successful business. Both of them benefited by the lesson of perseverance that sports offers. The main point is that you don't have to be a Hall of Fame athlete to reap the benefits of participating in sports.

In math class, I learned that the whole is equal to the sum of its parts. But that is not always the case when you are dealing with people. Sports has taught me that the whole is either greater than or less than the sum of its parts, depending on how well the parts work together. And how the parts work together depends on how they really understand the concept of teamwork.

Most people believe that teamwork is a fifty-fifty proposition. But true teamwork is seldom, if ever, fifty-fifty. Teamwork is *whatever it takes to get the job done.* There is no time for the measurement of contributions, no time for anything but concentrating on your job.

One year, my Pittsburgh Steelers were playing the Houston Oilers in the Astrodome late in the season, with the division championship on the line. Our offensive line was hard hit by the flu, our starting quarterback was out with an injury, and we were having difficulty making a first down. There was tremendous pressure on our defense to perform well—and they rose to the occasion. If the players on the defensive unit had been measuring their contribution against the offense's contribution, they would have given up and gone home. Instead, with a "whatever it takes" attitude, they increased their level of concentration and performance, forced turnovers, and got the ball into field goal range for our offense. Thanks to our defense's winning attitude, we came away with a victory.

Believing in doing whatever it takes to get the job done is what separates a successful person from someone who is not as successful. Nobody can give you this winning outlook; you have to develop it. And I know from experience that it can be learned and developed on the playing field.

My favorite people on the football field have always been offensive linemen and defensive backs. I say this because it takes special people to perform well in jobs in which there is little public recognition when they are doing things right but are thrust into the spotlight as soon as they make a mistake. That is exactly what happens to a lineman whose man sacks the quarterback or a defensive back who lets his receiver catch a touchdown pass. They know the importance of being part of a group that believes in teamwork and does not point fingers at one another.

Sports can be a learning situation as much as it can be fun. And that's why I say, "Get involved. Participate."

CHUCK NOLL, the Pittsburgh Steelers head coach from 1969–1991, led his team to four Super Bowl victories—the most by any coach. Widely respected as an innovator on both offense and defense, Noll was inducted into the Pro Football Hall of Fame in 1993.

1

SUPER BOWL SHUFFLE

On January 26, 1986, more than 73,000 fans packed the Louisiana Superdome in New Orleans for the 20th edition of the National Football League (NFL) Super Bowl. The Super Bowl was then—and is still—the number one sports extravaganza in the United States. For football fans, Super Sunday was the crowning moment of the year; for those who never watched a football game during the regular season, it was a chance to brighten up the winter months with a lively party. In 1986, the thousands in the stands and the 127 million people in front of their TVs awaited the opening kickoff with a special relish, because of the massive publicity generated by one of the competing teams—the Chicago Bears.

The Bears, known as the Monsters of the Midway, were one of pro football's most storied franchises. Throughout their 65-year history,

Star running back Walter Payton showed off his throwing form as if to prove how relaxed and confident the Bears were before Super Bowl XX.

they had played a rugged brand of football that was often called dirty by bruised and battered opponents. Their approach to the game reflected the image of Chicago itself, the bustling, wind-swept metropolis that poet Carl Sandburg had called the "city of big shoulders."

Unfortunately, the Bears had also come to represent another hometown sports tradition: failing to win championships despite excellent athletes who played their hearts out. In baseball, the Chicago Cubs had last won the World Series in 1908, and the Chicago White Sox had not won since 1917. Chicago's hockey team, the Black Hawks, had last captured the Stanley Cup in 1961. The Chicago Bulls had reached the National Basketball Association finals just once, in 1947. (However, with Michael Jordan now on the team, their history was about to change.)

The Bears themselves had enjoyed only one moment of glory following the end of World War II in 1945: an NFL championship in 1963. Since the creation of the Super Bowl in 1967, the Bears had never come close to earning a trip to football's biggest game. The team had featured some great individual talents, such as Dick Butkus, Mike Ditka, and Gayle Sayers, but these men had toiled and bled for losing teams. And for a long time it had looked as though the most recent Bears star—perhaps the greatest of them all—was doomed to continue this saga of futility.

The true fans watching the game, and the seasoned reporters who were gathered in the Superdome's press boxes, were well aware how much the game meant to Walter Payton. They had followed his exploits Sunday after Sunday for 11 seasons. They had seen him become the first player in NFL history to rush for 1,000 yards six years in a row. They had seen him set pro football's single-game rushing mark by slashing his way for 275 yards against one of the league's top defenses. They had seen him become the NFL's all-time leading rusher, racking up more than 14,000 yards in a career that was still going strong. They had seen him catch passes, throw passes, return kickoffs, and block with the power of a lineman. They had marveled at the ability of his 5'10", 205-pound frame to absorb the weekly pounding of pro football: Since joining the Bears in 1975, Payton had missed only one game due to injury. In short, they had seen Walter Payton do everything imaginable on the football field, except achieve every player's ultimate ambition—win a Super Bowl ring.

Standing in Payton's way were the New England Patriots, like the Bears making their first Super Bowl appearance. But unlike the Bears, who had enjoyed a spectacular 15-1 season, the Pats had not even won their division, making the playoffs as a wild-card team with 11 wins and 5 losses. Then they had caught fire, beating the New York Jets, the Oakland Raiders, and the Miami Dolphins to earn themselves the trip to New Orleans. Fans had to wonder if they were preparing a rerun of Super Bowl III, when quarterback Joe Namath had led the Jets to a shocking upset over the heavily favored Baltimore Colts.

The Bears never considered such a possibility. Otis Wilson, a linebacker, even predicted a shutout. The Bears were so confidant that shortly before the playoffs, Payton and a number of his teammates took time off to make a music video. Dressed in their uniforms, minus pads but sporting sunglasses, the brash Chicagoans had gleefully boogied and rapped their way through a number called "The Super Bowl Shuffle." When they arrived in New Orleans, many of the Bears stayed out late, sampling the city's legendary night life.

Most coaches would have immediately clamped down on such behavior, but Bears head coach Mike Ditka paid no attention to it. He was happy to let his players strut and brag to their hearts' content—as long as they were able to back it up on the field.

When the game finally started, the Bears quickly began to look like a team that had talked itself into oblivion. The first play from scrimmage went well enough: Quarterback Jim McMahon fittingly handed the ball to Payton, who ran off-tackle for a solid gain of seven yards. On second down, McMahon called Payton's number again but chose the wrong play for the alignment the Bears were in. Instead of sending Payton to the strong side, where the tight end could help seal off the corner, he had number 34 running a sweep to the more exposed weak side. New England's Garin Veris knifed in quickly from his defensive end position and nailed Payton before he could gain momentum; the ball squirted out of Payton's grasp, and linebacker Don Blackmon recovered deep in Bears territory. As Payton paced the sideline in anguish, New England quarterback Tony Eason narrowly missed connecting on a pass into the Chicago end zone. The Pats settled for a field goal and a 3-0 lead.

Moments later, McMahon, the cockiest of all the Bears, gave the Patriots another opening when he dropped back to his own 31 yardline and threw a pass into the flat. Once again, Blackmon was on the spot. The ball was coming right at him—he only needed to squeeze it and jog into the end zone.

Luckily for the Bears, McMahon's toss slid through Blackmon's hands, hit him in the chest, and bounced harmlessly to the turf. Given a reprieve from disaster, the feisty quarterback uncorked another pass and hit wide receiver Wille Gault for a 43-yard gain. The drive ended with the Bears kicking a field goal to tie the score.

The Patriots got the ball back. But the Bear's vaunted defense unleashed the most fearful campaign of physical domination yet seen in a Super Bowl. On New England's next three possessions, the team ran only nine plays, lost 22 yards, suffered two sacks, and coughed up two fumbles. By the middle of the second quarter, New England head coach Ray Berry pulled the shellshocked Eason from the game and replaced him with veteran Steve Grogan. The change did little good, as the Patriots ended the half with mind-boggling totals of minus 5 yards rushing and minus 14 passing.

Meanwhile, the Bears began to click on offense. Their game plan, which in previous years could have been expressed in five words—"Give the ball to Payton"—was now considerably more varied. Payton had gained more than 1,400

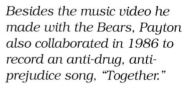

Besides the music video he made with the Bears, Payton also collaborated in 1986 to record an anti-drug, anti-prejudice song, "Together."

William "Refrigerator" Perry, the 320-pound defensive lineman, got to score a touchdown in the 1986 Super Bowl even though Payton did not. Jim McMahon celebrated the score.

yards during the regular season, and the Bears knew that the New England defense would have to key on him. In their Super Bowl scheme, therefore, they often employed Payton as a decoy: McMahon would fake a hand-off to Payton, drawing the defenders toward him, and then either throw to an open receiver or hand off to the Bears' number two back, Matt Suhey. After one of these textbook fakes, Suhey scored the Bears' first touchdown with an 11-yard run.

Following Suhey's score, the Bears poured it on mercilessly, turning the game into a 46-10 laugher. By the fourth quarter, the Bears were already celebrating on the sideline. One of the few exciting moments left for the TV audience was the sight of the chunky Payton making a tremendous leap in order to high-five Richard Dent, the Bears' 6'5" defensive end. It may have been the toughest play any Bear had to make that afternoon.

If life were a Hollywood movie, Payton would have capped his magnificent career by gaining 100-plus yards, scoring two or three touchdowns, and being named the most valuable player of the Super Bowl. The facts of the day were otherwise. Dent, who had spent much of the game in New England's backfield, was named the Super Bowl MVP, a rare but well-deserved honor for a stand-out defensive performance. On the offensive end, Payton had done nothing less than a solid day's work. Though he had not scored, he had carried the ball 22 times and gained 61 yards, making him the team's leading rusher. He had executed his fakes to perfection, diving into the line rather than simply pulling up, and he had blocked with his usual devastating effectiveness. He had shown football connoisseurs the all-around skills and dedication that had prompted Mike Ditka to call him "the very best football player I've ever seen, period—at any position." Most importantly, he had helped his team win, and gotten what he came for—a Super Bowl ring.

As the jubilant Bears whooped it up in their locker room after the game, Payton was observed lighting a victory cigar for his close friend and running mate Matt Suhey. When Suhey passed the cigar back, Payton took one puff and started coughing. A reporter asked him if it was his first cigar. "Yes," Payton replied, "and it will be the last. Until next year."

During the season, Suhey had spoken about Payton's motivation: "One thing he's often said is, he's got the records, he's got a good life, he's made a lot of money out of this, but he hasn't got the ultimate accomplishment: To win the Super Bowl."

Payton had finally reached his goal. In actual distance, the scene of his triumph was only about 80 miles from his boyhood home in Mississippi. But the road he had traveled to reach the Super Bowl had been much, much longer.

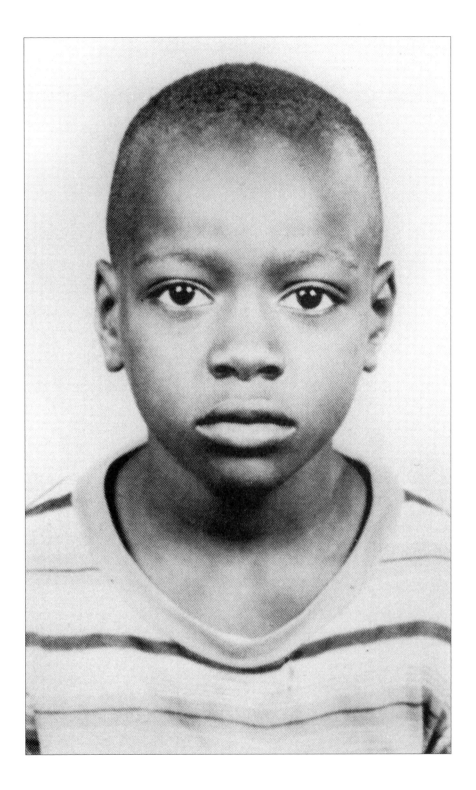

2

YOU LEARN SOME GOOD MOVES

Walter Jerry Payton was born in Columbia, Mississippi, on July 25, 1954. Walter later called the area where he grew up "a kid's paradise." On one side of his house there were woods leading to the Pearl River, on the other side, a group of factories. Both settings provided endless opportunities for exploring and mischief.

Walter's father, Peter, worked for a firm that manufactured packs and parachutes for the U.S. government. The Paytons were not poor, but the family lived simply. Any extra money was put aside for the new house that Peter and Alyne Payton hoped to build.

One of Walter's favorite pastimes was to play hide and seek with his older siblings Eddie and Pamela. They and their friends went to a nearby pickle factory, dunking one another in the vats of brine and trying to avoid being nabbed by the security guard. Walter's natural running ability came in handy during these escapades, but

Payton was called Bubba, short for big-eyed boy, when he was young.

sometimes he did not run fast enough. "Whenever I got caught after one of my pranks, there was no place to hide from my daddy," he wrote in his autobiography, *Sweetness*. "He was one good disciplinarian. He didn't cut just one switch. He cut two or three in case he wore out the first ones before he was through. And often he did."

The strongest memory Walter retained from childhood was his parents' love and concern, whippings and all: "My parents spent a lot of time with us and made us feel loved and wanted. I didn't care much about what went on around me, as long as I was in solid at home."

In 1962, when Walter was eight, Peter and Alyne Payton were able to afford the house they had dreamed of. The new home—which contained a separate room for each of the Payton children—was located just a block from John J. Jefferson High School, which all the local black children attended from grade 1 through grade 12. Racial segregation was still the norm in Mississippi, but Walter never let it disturb him. His sense of pride was due in large part to his father, who, he recalled, "taught me never to settle for second-best, that either you tried to do your best or don't try at all. And he always made sure that if we started something, we finished it."

Walter applied that approach to school and became a better-than-average student, though he was not above slipping away to his nearby home at odd times during the day. He loved to dance and bang out rhythms on anything within reach. The constant drumming was a trial to his mother, and Walter's fun-loving attitude did not always sit well with Eddie and Pamela. "People ask, 'Where did you get all of those shifty moves,'" he recalled in 1993 when he was inducted into the Football Hall of Fame. "And the answer is that I was the baby in the family. When my mom would leave us home and tell us to have the house clean by the time she got back, my older brother and sister had to do all the cleaning. And when you've got an angry brother and sister chasing you with a broom and a wet towel, well, you learn some good moves."

Football was not on Walter's agenda as he entered ninth grade. He went out for the track team and became an excellent long jumper, but his main interest was playing the drums in the Jefferson band.

Some of Walter's avoidance of football had to do with his brother, Eddie, who was a star halfback on the Jefferson team. Walter later claimed that he had stayed off the team because he did not want his mother worrying about both her sons getting hurt. However, Alyne Payton later offered a different theory. "Eddie is a real talker," she explained, "but Walter has always been sort of quiet, sort of off by himself. Eddie used to tell Walter all sorts of things about football—what to do here, how to do this and that—and I think Walter sort of resented it."

When Eddie Payton graduated, Charles "Ham" Boston, Jefferson's football coach, asked Walter to try out for the team. The sophomore said OK, only after being promised he could stay in the band.

Walter had the speed and agility to play halfback, but at first he was leery about getting hit. As a result, he would run wherever he saw day-

A view of Walter Payton's home football field. In high school, Payton played his heart out not only as a football player, but as a drummer in the band. "I loved the big sound, the beat, the rhythm, the action," he said.

light instead of following the design of the play.

As Payton recalled, Coach Boston solved the problem by telling him to punish the tacklers: "In other words, why should I be the only one who gets clobbered?" Once he had that principle down, Walter was ready to go. On his first official run from scrimmage, he scampered 65 yards for a touchdown. In a game later in the season, Walter scored 6 touchdowns and a 2-point conversion for a total of 38 points, as his team won, 42-0.

When Walter entered his junior year in 1969, Jefferson was combined with the previously all-white Columbia High School, and Walter became Columbia's undisputed star. "Whenever we needed points, he was the man," coach Tommy Davis later said. Walter scored in every game during his junior and senior years and led the Little Dixie Conference in scoring as a senior. He was named to the all-conference team three years in a row and made the all-state team as a senior. However, as a foretaste of frustrations to come, Columbia failed to win the conference championship.

In addition to his football heroics, Walter turned in a personal best of 22'11¼" in the long jump, averaged 18 points a game for Columbia's basketball team, and even played some baseball. He continued to drum in the band and later claimed to have been the best (and flashiest) cymbals player in the state of Mississippi.

During his senior year, Walter was recruited by a number of colleges, and he finally narrowed his choice down to Kansas State University and nearby Jackson State College. Feeling that he needed to get away from home, he signed a letter of intent with Kansas State. But as the beginning of the school year drew closer, Walter began to have second thoughts. He agonized for quite a while and finally asked his mother to make the choice for him. Not surprisingly, she decided that he should stay close to Columbia. In the fall of 1971, Walter packed his bags and made the 90-mile trip to Jackson, Mississippi, where he would truly mature as a football player and as a man.

3
A TIGER NAMED SWEETNESS

By agreeing to attend Jackson State, Walter proved that he was no longer intimidated by his older brother. Indeed, he roomed with Eddie, and with Edward "Sugar Bear" Moses, another player from Columbia, and later said, "I think playing alongside my friends and my brother was one of the reasons I learned to be a good blocker. When they were out there sacrificing themselves so I could gain a few more yards, I wanted to do the same for them."

Walter's unique talents immediately impressed head coach Bob Hill. Hill, a tough disciplinarian, wanted things done his way or not at all. For example, he always demanded that his running backs come up out of their stance with a crossover step. Walter, however, was more comfortable lifting his front foot first. To everyone's amazement, Hill allowed him to keep on doing it. "Okay, everybody, I want you to do it this way," he would tell the backs; looking at

It didn't take long before Payton became Jackson State College's star athlete.

Walter, he would add, "And you, fool, you do it your way."

Walter soon earned a starting position in the backfield alongside Eddie. The brothers' most memorable game came against Alabama A & M in the Azalea Classic on Thanksgiving Day. "He'd sweep one way and then I'd sweep the other," Walter recalled. "They didn't know which Payton would hit 'em next or from which side." Playing other predominantly black schools such as Texas Southern, Grambling, Morgan State, and Alcorn A & M, the Tigers compiled an excellent 9-1-1 record. Walter had a solid debut season, rushing for 614 yards on 80 carries, an impressive 7.6 average.

The brothers' tandem team did not last long. Eddie graduated in 1971 and embarked on a pro football career. If Walter missed his big brother, he didn't demonstrate it on the field. In the Tigers' second game, a 72-0 trouncing of Lane College, Payton scored seven touchdowns (equaling his previous year's total) and a pair of 2-point conversions, for a total of 46 points—the highest single-game performance in the history of college football. Jackson State ended the season in a tie for first place in the Southwestern Athletic Conference (SWAC). Payton, doing double duty as a place kicker, was the second leading scorer in the nation with 117 points (16 TDs and 21 PATs).

Around this time, Payton acquired the nickname Sweetness. Some say it was inspired by his sweet moves on the field; others claim that it arose from Payton's sincerity and genuine humility. Payton had been raised as a devout Baptist, and he always led the football team in prayer before games. He often expressed his desire to help those less fortunate than himself. "I wanted my life to mean something more than a bunch of numbers on paper, newspaper clippings, and standing ovations," he recalled.

Payton could be serious and hardworking, but he still possessed the explosive energy that had sometimes exasperated his family. "The whole team would be standing in the parking lot on campus waiting for the bus to the stadium," Coach Hill recalled. "Some guys would start playing music and Walter would dance for a good half hour sometimes. He'd put pads on, jump up, and land on his elbows and knees. He'd do flips and everything. He was only pumping himself up, but it scared me. I couldn't stand to watch."

Hill had no trouble watching as Payton tore up the SWAC throughout his junior year. He ripped off 1,139 yards on the ground and led the nation in scoring with 160 points, as the Tigers again won a share of the SWAC crown. Payton was voted the conference's MVP and named to the Black All-America Team.

Was Payton content with his success? No. During the summer, he went back to Columbia and worked on a new training program with his brother. In the intense heat, they ran 65-yard sprints through the sand along the Pearl River and quick dashes up 45-degree embankments. "We had guys come from all over to train," Eddie Payton recalled, "and we carried more of them off than could walk away when we finished." The grueling workouts increased Walter's unusual leg strength and gave him the ability to change direction at full speed without losing his balance.

Payton returned to Jackson a better player, but the Tigers posted a less than stellar 7-3 record, and Payton's senior stats were a shade below those of his previous year. Even so, he had become the all-time leading career scorer in NCAA history with 464 points: in addition to his 66 touchdowns, he had booted 5 field goals and 53 extra points. As a runner, he had gained 3,563 yards, for a spectacular average of 6.1 yards per carry. If that were not enough, he had thrown 19 passes on the halfback option play, completing 14 for 4 touchdowns. He had also been the team's punter, averaging 39 yards per kick, and had posted a remarkable 43-yard average on kickoff returns.

Payton completed his B.A. in special education in only three and a half years and began working toward his master's degree. One reason he hit the books so hard, he later wrote, was "to help dispel the myth that athletes in general and black athletes in particular don't have to work to get their diplomas and that they don't learn anything anyway."

Playing for a small, predominantly black school deprived Payton of any chance at winning the coveted Heisman Trophy. He made the Black All-America Team for the second year in a row and also made the NCAA Division II All-America Team. Payton played in the East-West Shrine Game and the Senior Bowl, and he was chosen for the College All-Star Team. A number of NFL teams had been scouting him diligently, and when the 1975 NFL draft rolled around, the Chicago Bears made him their first-round pick, the fourth player chosen overall.

Payton was not excited by being taken so high in the draft. "I guess that's just the way I am," he explained. "Even being named to the All-American teams was sort of anticlimactic.

The doing and achieving is the true success, not being rewarded for it once it has been done." Instead, Payton was more excited about his relationship with Connie Norwood, a young woman from New Orleans introduced to Payton by Coach Hill. The two had "clicked," as Payton put it, and they would soon get engaged.

Displaying the keen business sense that marked his subsequent career, Payton retained an attorney to help negotiate his contract with the Bears. Payton wanted a bonus larger than the one Archie Manning received when he signed with the New Orleans Saints in 1971. Manning had quarterbacked for the University of Mississippi, a school that had been closed to blacks while Payton was growing up. Walter was eager to bring added prestige to Jackson State (by then a full-fledged university). The Bears agreed to pay $126,000, the highest figure ever for a player from the state of Mississippi, and Payton was on his way north to Chicago.

Walter Payton holds the trophy given him in 1975 for being named Football Roundup's *College Player of the Year. With him is Coach Bob Hill.*

4

MONSTERS OF
THE MIDWAY

In the summer of 1975, when Payton arrived
at the Chicago Bears training camp in Lake For-
est, Illinois, he was joining one of the great franchises in pro football. The Bears had been cre-
ated in 1920 by a pair of football stars from the
University of Illinois, George Halas and Dutch
Sternaman. Halas eventually became the team's
sole owner and was one of the founders of the
National Football League. He also coached the
team until 1968, by which time he was known
simply as Papa Bear.

From their origin until 1970, the Bears had
played their games in Cubs Park (renamed
Wrigley Field during the 1920s), the home of
Chicago's National League baseball team. In that
setting, with the double-decked stands over-
hanging the field and the wind whipping in off
Lake Michigan, Chicagoans had seen many of
football's all-time greats perform their heroics:
Bronko Nagurski, Red Grange, Joe Stydahar,

*Red Grange helped create the Chicago Bears' tradi-
tion of greatness.*

Payton not only was Chicago's star running back and pass catcher, he also excelled at returning kickoffs.

Bulldog Turner, George McAfee, Ed Sprinkle, Sid Luckman, Johnny Lujack, George Blanda, Doug Atkins, and Bill George were among the immortals who had worn the midnight blue of the Bears. The dominant team of the NFL's first two decades, the Bears reached their absolute peak in the 1940 championship game, when they trounced the Washington Redskins by the almost incredible score of 73-0.

After that high-water mark, the Bears continued to be a tough and colorful team, and their hard-hitting (and sometimes downright vicious) contests with midwestern rivals such as the Detroit Lions and the Green Bay Packers became the stuff of football legend. But however hard the Bears played the game, someone else usually finished with a better record. In the decades following World War II, Halas's men captured only one championship, and even that came hard: on a brutally cold December afternoon in 1963, the Bears survived a desperate struggle with the New York Giants on the frozen turf of Wrigley Field, coming away with a 14-10 victory.

In 1970, the team moved its home games to the more spacious Soldier Field. The move did little to inspire the Bears, who had fallen on hard times since their 1963 NFL title. During the late 1960s and early 1970s, the Bears had continued to showcase brilliant individual performers. Dick Butkus dominated the field from his middle linebacker spot, making tackles that sounded like streetcar wrecks. Tight end Mike Ditka snagged every pass thrown in his direction and routinely bulled his way downfield with tacklers hanging onto him. Halfback Gale Sayers put on a highlight-film performance game after game, displaying moves that left spectators and defenders gasping in disbelief.

Despite the exploits of these future Hall of Famers, the Bears were more likely to come up losers than winners on any given Sunday. The team's overall record between 1963 and 1974 was below .500, and 1975 did not promise to be much better. Butkus, Ditka, and Sayers were all gone. By making Payton their number one pick and paying him a healthy bonus, the Bears had clearly tabbed him as a building block for the team's future. The Chicago press was already hailing the rookie halfback as "the new Gale Sayers" before he had even played a down.

Payton was not thrilled to have that kind of pressure put on him. Both he and the Bears began the 1975 campaign slowly. The team lost six of its first seven games, scoring a total of only 57 points. Payton, slowed by an infected elbow and a bruised leg and ankle, was the second-string halfback, behind Mike Adamle. He had little to show for his efforts beyond a 95-yard day against the Philadelphia Eagles in the Bears' lone win and, in a 46-13 thrashing administered by the Minnesota Vikings, his first NFL touchdown. "At this point," he said later, "the best thing about professional football was the money."

The Bears did manage to win three of their last seven games. With his injuries completely healed, Payton gave the Chicago fans a sample of what he could do for the team. In a 42-17 victory over the New Orleans Saints, he rushed for 134 yards (including a 54-yard TD run), caught 5 passes for another 62 yards, and ran back a pair of kickoffs for 104 yards—a total of 300 yards. He finished the season with 679 rushing yards, the most for a Bears back since Sayers's 1,032 in 1969. Nevertheless, he considered his rookie year a disappointment.

In the summer of 1976, Connie Norwood graduated from Jackson State, and on July 7, she and Payton were married. The event boosted Payton's spirits considerably. "Besides making me totally happy with myself for the only time in my life that I could remember," he recalled, "I knew Connie would be another settling element in Chicago during the season."

In 1976, the Bears made Payton the focal point of their running game. He carried the ball 311 times and racked up 1,390 yards. The Bears entered the last game of the season, against the

Denver Broncos, with a 7-6 record, and Payton was vying with the Buffalo Bill's O. J. Simpson for the league rushing title. The Bears jumped out to a 14-0 lead, but the Broncos held Payton to just 41 yards in the first half. In the third quarter, Payton sprained his ankle and had to leave the game. He sat on the sideline in tears, watching the Bears go down by a score of 28-14. Meanwhile, Simpson was having a big day against the Baltimore Colts. Most people assumed that Payton was crying over the loss of the rushing title, but he actually felt worse about the team's failure to achieve a winning season. Nevertheless, the Bears' 7-7 record marked the first time they had finished at .500 since 1968.

During the off-season, Payton went back to Mississippi to continue his graduate work in special education, still tormented by the idea that he had not done his job. According to Mike Adamle, "It got to the point where he felt he was carrying the whole team, that he had to have a great run every time he got the ball."

When Payton reported to training camp, observers noted that he was not as high-spirited as he had been in the past. There were times when he even seemed downright irritable, and before the Bears' first regular-season game, he refused to talk with reporters. Speculation about his moodiness was put to rest during the coming months—he had merely been preparing himself mentally for one of the greatest individual seasons in the history of football.

In a 1977 pre-season game, Walter (right) played against his brother Eddie, then with the Cleveland Browns.

Payton started the 1977 season by rushing for 160 yards against the Detroit Lions. After nine games the Bears stood only at 4-5, but Payton was burning up the league: He had already gained 1,129 yards, and some people felt that he had a shot at cracking O. J. Simpson's single-season rushing mark of 2,003.

Payton chalked up his first 200-yard game against the Green Bay Packers on the seventh week of the season, and it appeared that he would need two or three more if he was going to hit 2,000. He came close in his ninth game, tearing off 192 against the Kansas City Chiefs. But he was facing a tough challenge in the Bears' 10th game, to be played in Minnesota on November 20 against the division-leading Vikings, one of the league's toughest defensive teams. To his frustration, Payton came down with a case of the flu during the week. He was barely able to

The Vikings had been to the Super Bowl in three of the past four years, but on November 20, 1977, they could not stop Walter Payton.

practice, and Bears coach Jack Pardee told the press that Payton would see limited duty at best.

Payton was still feeling feverish at game time, but the day was sunny and crisp, ideal football weather, and he was not inclined to sit on the bench and watch. On the Bears' first play from scrimmage, quarterback Bob Avellini decided to see how much Payton had to give and called for number 34 to carry the ball on a sweep. Payton rambled for 29 yards. Avellini kept on calling his number, and Payton kept on running. In the second quarter, with the ball on the Minnesota 15, Avellini continued to hand off to Payton. On his fourth straight carry, Payton cracked the goal line.

At the half, Payton had gained 144 yards, and the Bears led 10-0. Again and again the call went to Payton, and each time he fought his way for valuable real estate. Late in the fourth quarter, with the Bears clinging to a 10-7 lead, he had carried the ball 37 times and gained 210 yards. But he was far from finished. With the ball on Chicago's 33, he deftly avoided a pile-up at the line of scrimmage, cut to his right, took off down the sideline, and sprinted all the way to the Minnesota 9—a gain of 58 yards.

That run put the flu-ridden star only five yards away from Simpson's single-game rushing record of 273. He got the ball yet again and ran left for three yards. And then, on his 40th carry of the day, he bulled his way to the 2 yardline, dragging three tacklers with him. The gain of four gave him 275 yards on the day. Moments later, the final gun went off. The Bears had a hard-fought 10-7 win, and Payton had the record.

Suddenly, Payton was a national celebrity. Reporters clamored for interviews; the Hall of Fame asked for his jersey. With four games remaining in the schedule, fans across the country were eager to see if football's newest star, whose total had now reached 1,404, could bump Simpson from the record books.

Payton gave it all he had. Gaining 137, 101, and 163 yards in his next three games, he approached the final game of the season, against the New York Giants, needing 204 yards to break the record. As soon as Payton looked out the window on the morning of December 18, he understood that the quest was over. Freezing rain was falling, and the artificial surface of Giants Stadium was going to be a nightmare. "The sole concern now," Payton recalled, "was to figure out how to beat the Giants in their own stadium on a terrible day."

With players slipping and sliding all over the icy field, the game was tied 3-3 at the half. The Bears went up by 9-6 in the fourth quarter, but the Giants kicked a field goal to send the game into overtime. Payton had gained only 47 yards in regulation time, and he got nothing during overtime. But with the clock running down, the Bears mounted a last-ditch drive that was capped by a short pass to Payton, who slithered for 14 yards to the Giants 11. Bob Thomas kicked a field goal—and the Bears had their first winning season in 10 years and their first playoff berth in 14 years.

Payton ended the season with 1,852 yards, well short of the record. He admitted that he would have liked to crack 2,000 yards, but he liked being in the playoffs even better. "I'll take

Coming in to the last game of 1977, Payton had a chance to break the season-rushing record. But an inch of slush on the field made it hard to walk, let alone run.

those 14 yards on that pass play over any rushing record," he asserted.

The Bears' long-awaited return to postseason play was not a happy one, as the Dallas Cowboys, the eventual Super Bowl winners, crushed them by a score of 37-7. Dallas stacked its defense to stop Chicago's running game, and Payton managed only 61 yards on 19 carries. After the game, Dallas coach Tom Landry also singled him out. "You really don't appreciate a Walter Payton until you are on the sidelines against him. We were hitting him with two and three men."

With his compact body and powerful legs, Payton did not have the fluid grace of a Sayers or a Simpson. He tended to run on his toes, with short, stiff-legged strides, prancing and juking until he saw an opening. Though he could cover 40 yards in 4.5 seconds, he was not really a breakaway threat; lacking that mysterious extra gear in the open field, he could be caught from behind by fleet defensive backs. But no other halfback ever combined speed, shiftiness, and raw power the way Payton did. When he ran out of running room, he simply lowered his head and shoulders like a fullback and battered his way for extra yards. He loved to level a blitzing linebacker or throw a crisp lead block for another running back. No matter how hard he was hit, he popped up from the ground like a jack-in-the-box, eager for more.

Sweetness never glorified himself by spiking the ball after scoring a touchdown but instead handed the pigskin to one of his linemen: "They're the ones who do all the work," he explained. Payton's fondness for practical jokes though irked many Bears players and coaches. Every now and then, an official untangling a heap of players would suddenly find his shoelaces untied: Payton, having nothing to do at the bottom of the pile-up, had decided to have some fun.

During the off-season, the nation's football writers officially confirmed Payton's newfound status when they voted him the NFL's most valuable player. At age 23, Payton was the youngest man ever to win that honor. And as far as he was concerned, he was just getting started.

6

I'M STILL REACHING

During the winter of 1978, Payton sat down to talk business with the Bears management, and signed three one-year contracts that reflected his unquestioned status as a super-star. He was to be paid $400,000 for the 1978 season, $425,000 in 1979, and $450,000 plus incentive bonuses in 1980. The Bears were clearly a team on the rise; having reached the playoffs for the first time in 10 years, they were preparing to challenge for the NFC Central crown and the ultimate prize cherished by every team and player in pro football, a Super Bowl championship.

However, the way is never smooth for Chicago teams. During the off-season, Jack Pardee accepted an offer to become the head coach of the Washington Redskins and took most of his staff with him. Thus the Bears went into the season

Payton's success over the many years of his career was due in part to his ability to avoid getting hurt. Here a stiff arm against Oakland's Monte Jackson left the defender groping.

The arrival of quarterback Jim McMahon was a major factor in the improvement of the Chicago Bears during the mid-1980s.

adjusting to a new coaching staff, headed by Neill Armstrong, and a new system.

Not surprisingly, the Bears took a step backward, falling to 7-9 in the NFL's first 16-game season. Payton, adjusting to a revised running game that had him going up the middle more, also slipped from his exalted MVP numbers, but he still gained 1,395 yards, enough for the National Football Conference (NFC) rushing title, and caught 50 passes for another 480 yards. (Earl Campbell, playing for the Houston Oilers in the American Conference, won the first of his three consecutive NFL rushing titles with 1,450 yards.)

No other runner in Bears history had ever put together three straight 1,000-yard seasons. Fullback Roland Harper chipped in with 992 yards, and together the two backs, who were close friends off the field, accounted for 72 percent of Chicago's offensive output.

The 1979 season began gloomily for the Bears as Harper went down with a knee injury, but the improving team managed a 10-6 finish and a wild-card berth in the playoffs. Payton logged 1,610 yards on the ground despite a pinched nerve in his shoulder, leading the NFC for the fourth straight year. He put on a show in the Bears' playoff contest with the Philadelphia Eagles, scoring two touchdowns in the first half as the Bears went up by a score of 17-10. In the third quarter, Payton broke loose on an 84-yard gallop, the longest run of his career. But the play was wiped out by an illegal-motion penalty; for the first time anyone could recall, Payton stayed on the ground after being tackled, pounding the turf in frustration. The Bears' luck had turned again: The Eagles came back to win the game, 27-17.

The disappointment carried over into 1980, when the Bears slipped back to 7-9, despite another 1,460 yards from Payton, good enough for his fifth straight NFC rushing crown. The following year, the Bears dropped six of their first seven games and struggled to a 6-10 finish. Even Payton—who played most of the season with cracked ribs and a sore shoulder—resembled a mere mortal as he slipped to seventh place in the NFL rushing list with 1,222 yards. He even failed to make the Pro Bowl for once, but the Bears appreciated him all the same—during the off-season, Payton signed a three-year contract worth $2 million.

The Bears appeared to be mired in futility, and owner George Halas and general manager Jim Finks decided to shake things up by bringing in Mike Ditka as the new head coach. Anticipation ran high, but the 1982 season was crippled by a players' strike that lasted nearly two months. The teams played only nine games apiece, and the Bears, a team in transition, lost all but three. The only bright spot for Payton came when he passed the 10,000-yard mark for his career during a game against the Rams in Los Angeles. Characteristically, he was somewhat embarrassed when the officials stopped the game so that the crowd could recognize his achievement. "I felt like I wanted them to hurry up and get it out of the way," he confessed. "I wanted to be doing what we're supposed to be doing."

The Bears, who added half a dozen talented rookies in a splendid 1983 draft, were supposed to start winning under Ditka. However, the season began on a sad note due to the death of George Halas at the age of 88, and the team struggled through its first 10 games, going 3-7. The season turned around when Ditka—who had broken his hand when he punched a steel locker after one loss—decided to go with second-year man Jim McMahon at quarterback. The Bears promptly won five of their last six games, ending the season at .500. Throughout all the turmoil, Payton worked at his job week after week, and he wound up with 1,421 yards, fourth best in the NFL. He also led the league in pass receptions with 53. During the off-season, the Chicago management renegotiated Payton's contract, making him the highest-paid player in NFL history.

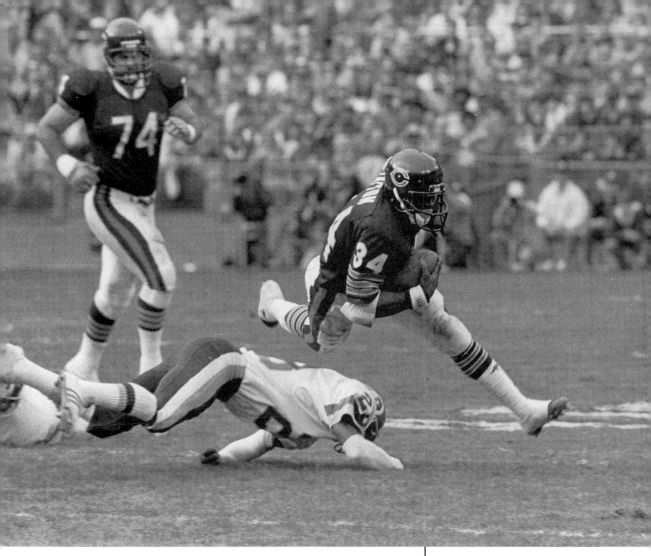

Payton was being well compensated for his efforts, but more than anything he wanted to play for a winning team. Nevertheless, as the 1984 season got under way, his individual achievements were in the spotlight. He was closing in on the NFL's all-time career rushing record of 12,312 yards, established by the great Cleveland Browns fullback Jim Brown. Brown had retired after the 1965 season, and in the nearly 20 years since then only Franco Harris of the Pittsburgh Steelers had come close to challenging his record. As long as Payton stayed

Payton enjoyed winning the playoff game against the Washington Redskins in 1984 even more than setting the record for most rushing yards in a career.

healthy, he was certain to overtake Brown by midseason.

In rolling over the Tampa Bay Buccaneers and Denver Broncos to start the season, the Bears made it clear that they wanted Payton to get the record quickly. The rapidly maturing offensive line, powered by center Jay Hilgenberg, guards Mark Bortz and Kurt Becker, and tackles Keith Van Horne and Jim Covert, blasted huge holes for Payton and fullback Matt Suhey. In the Denver game, Payton enjoyed one of his finest afternoons, gaining 179 yards on just 20 carries, including the longest touchdown run of his career, a 62-yarder. Going into the season's fourth game, against the Saints in New Orleans, Payton needed just over 100 yards to break Brown's record.

As the media homed in on the October 7 game, some commentators were ready to enshrine Payton as the greatest running back of all time, but he was impatient with such talk. "Numbers don't indicate the greatness of a man or his accomplishments," he told reporters. "They don't tell if he has reached all his expectations. . . . I have always tried to maintain a level of dedication, plus a willingness not to settle for the best, but to reach beyond my last performance. I'm still going. I'm still reaching."

Having put things in perspective, he then turned in his 59th 100-yard game and became the NFL's all-time leading rusher. Even better from Payton's point of view, the Bears won their division with a 10-6 record and then beat the Washington Redskins in the playoffs, 23-19, in a vintage Payton game: he ran for 104 yards, threw a 19-yard touchdown pass, and knocked a Washington defensive back out of the game with a thunderous block.

The Bears then traveled to San Francisco for the NFC title game, only to be shut out, 23-0, by a superbly prepared 49ers team. Payton had another productive day, gaining 92 yards on the ground and catching 3 passes, but he was devastated by the loss, calling it "the hardest thing I ever had to deal with." He had been one step from the Super Bowl, and everything had crumbled. He went back to Chicago in a dismal mood, not realizing that the best was yet to come.

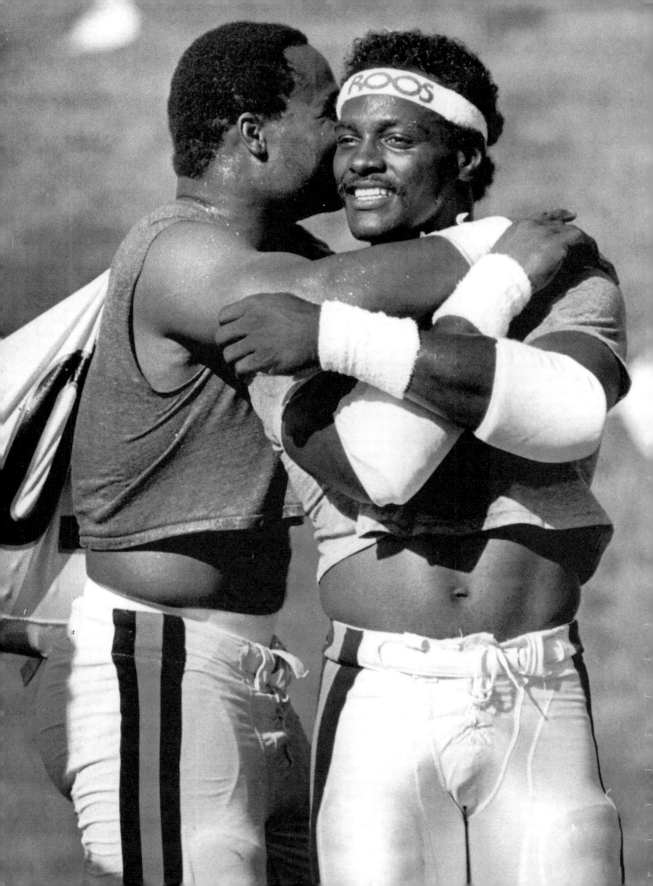

7

HE'S IN HIS GLORY NOW

By the time training camp began in 1985, Payton had recovered his high spirits and was playing his usual practical jokes. His teammates had also drawn new resolve from their disaster in San Francisco and the criticism they had taken during the summer. "We're a team with something to prove," said all-pro defensive tackle Dan Hampton. Linebacker Otis Wilson was even more emphatic: "We're on a mission," he declared.

With that attitude, the Bears had the final ingredient they needed to dominate the NFL. Jim McMahon, who had missed the end of the season and the playoffs in 1984 with a lacerated kidney, was back as the starting quarterback. Mike Ditka, realizing that the Bears had been too predictable, decided to open up the offense and feature the pass as much as the run. Defensive coordinator Buddy Ryan had developed a superb nucleus of players for his aggressive "46" defense: in addition to Hampton and Wilson, he

Mike Singletary (left) hugged Payton during the 1985 training camp—a sign of how close the Bears were.

had defensive linemen Richard Dent and Steve McMichael, linebackers Mike Singletary and Wilber Marshall, and defensive backs Gary Fencik, Dave Duerson, and Mike Richardson—all among the very best in the league at their positions.

Right out of the chute, the Bears began to steamroll everyone in their way. They not only won—they took the field with an attitude of contempt for the opposition, and they were not shy about saying so. After the Green Bay Packers complained that the Bears had tried to run up the score in the longtime rivals' first meeting of the season, Ditka snarled, "If they don't like it, let them do something about it in two weeks." The public, accustomed to hearing players and coaches droning on about their respect for the opposition, lapped it up.

As the Chicago Bears crunched their way to a 15-1 record (losing only to the Miami Dolphins, in the 13th week of the season), a host of colorful characters emerged to claim the limelight. Ditka

Payton was a fierce blocker, as Dolphin linebacker Hugh Green learned the hard way.

and the equally strong-willed Ryan, often clash-
ing over strategy, were always ready to snipe at
one another in the media. McMahon, a free-
wheeling character who butted heads with teammates after touchdowns, developed the mystique
of a rock star. William "The Refrigerator" Perry,
the mountainous 300-pound defensive lineman
who was said to devour three or four chickens at
a sitting, became the darling of every out-of-
shape TV watcher in America. It was easy to
overlook Walter Payton, who just went out every
week and got his 100 yards, quietly chugging
along toward the Football Hall of Fame.

Payton's teammates never forgot him for a
moment. Quite simply, they were awed by him.
They had seen him in the weight room, bench-
pressing 390 pounds and leg-pressing more
than 600. In practice, he could throw a football
60 yards, punt for 70 yards, and boot 45-yard
field goals. When he was in the mood, he would
walk the width of the field on his hands. People
who slapped him on the back felt like they were
touching a brick wall.

The Bears were equally amazed by Payton's
durability, his dedication, and his passion for
the game. "Walter plays with the enthusiasm of
a 10th-grader," Dan Hampton marveled. "You
see a lot of players who are jaded on the job. Yet
here's one of the greatest of all time, and he's
still trying to be the best tailback on the 10th-
grade team." Payton worked out just as hard in
the off-season as he had when he was in college: whereas most players showed up in training camp ready to get into shape, Payton showed
up ready to play football.

Those who knew him best scoffed at some
reporters' suggestions that Payton was not the

player he once was or that he missed being the focal point of the team's attack. "I hear people say he's lost a step," Matt Suhey commented. "That's pure bull. He's absolutely as good as he's ever been. Probably, he is contributing as much as he ever has, but he doesn't always have the ball doing it. He picks up blitzes, blocks, runs great pass patterns. He's not frustrated. He's in his glory now."

Though Payton's number of carries had declined, his production had in fact gone up. During the season, he set a new NFL record by reeling off eight straight 100-yard games. His importance was highlighted when the Bears took their revenge on the 49ers on October 13. Typical of their new style, the Bears put the ball in the air on 15 of their first 20 plays and scored on their first four possessions. But when San Francisco narrowed the gap to 19-10 late in the fourth quarter, it was Payton time. "Payton carried nine times on a 13-play drive," wrote a local journalist. "He gained 52 of the 66 yards, and carried two defenders the last three yards on his 17-yard touchdown run with 3:41 left." After the game, Dan Hampton remarked, "I don't care how well McMahon plays. Payton's still the heart and soul of that offense."

The Bears had found their winning formula, and it carried them through the playoffs to their smashing 46-10 triumph in Super Bowl XX. The long-suffering Chicago fans finally had a championship team, and Walter Payton, who had once seemed doomed to play for also-rans, had his Super Bowl ring.

Even in the victors' locker room, reporters would not let go of the idea that Payton was unhappy—this time because he had failed to score a Super Bowl touchdown. "It doesn't matter," he insisted, but when he disappeared for half an hour and then left the Superdome quickly and quietly, his moodiness was carefully noted. During the off-season, writer Charles Siebert rekindled the issue, and Payton finally opened up a bit. "It wasn't the touchdown," he explained. "The game was dull."

The attitude was vintage Payton. He had wanted not merely to win the Super Bowl. He had wanted to be in thick of the hardest-fought Super Bowl of all time, a game that stretched his talents to the limit—and he would have been just as happy throwing a block to set up the winning touchdown as he would have been taking the ball in himself.

8

NEW HORIZONS

Payton had once suggested that he might get bored after reaching 15,000 yards. He breezed by that milestone during the second game of the 1986 season, but he showed no sign of losing interest in football. The Bears gave every indication of returning to the Super Bowl, compiling a 14-2 record. Payton was in his usual form, gaining 1,333 yards and catching 37 passes. But the Bears took a tumble in the playoffs, as the Washington Redskins beat them soundly at Soldier Field, 27-13.

Payton appeared quite capable of shooting for 20,000 yards, but he refused to look beyond 1987, and the season turned out to be one of the least inspiring vistas in NFL history. After the second game, the players went on strike over the issue of free agency, and the owners retaliated by playing three weeks' worth of dismal games with hastily assembled pickup squads.

On December 20, 1987, the crowd gave Payton a standing ovation before his final game at Chicago's Soldier Field.

When the players returned after a month's absence, bitter feelings lingered. The Bears managed a respectable 11-4 record, but again they lost to the Redskins in the playoffs.

Payton had spent the season splitting the halfback duties with talented newcomer Walter Anderson, gaining 533 yard and catching 33 passes. Taking stock, he decided it was time to bow out and let Anderson try to become the next Walter Payton. Payton's career achievements were truly staggering. He had amassed 16,726 rushing yards, nearly 4,000 more than the second player on the all-time list, Dallas's Tony Dorsett. He also owned the NFL career record for combined yards (rushing and pass receiving) with a total of 21,736. He had the most rushing touchdowns (110), most 1,000-yard seasons (10), and most 100-yard games (77) of any running back in history. He also owned 26 Chicago Bears records. Looking at his numbers, it was easy to understand why Dan Hampton had once said, "No one on this football team and no one in the NFL is actually in Walter Payton's league."

That was the opinion of a friend and teammate, but it was echoed by commentators who had no special allegiance to either Payton or the Bears. John Madden, former coach of the Oakland Raiders and the nation's number one football broadcaster, was equally emphatic about Payton's dominance. "Too many people judge a running back only by how many rushing yards he has," Madden wrote in his book *One Knee Equals Two Feet*. "You seldom hear how many passes a running back caught for how many yards. And you hardly ever hear how good a blocker he is, either as a pass blocker picking up a blitzing linebacker or as a run blocker for the other running back. But that's how coaches evaluate a running back. And that's why Walter Payton is the best running back I've ever seen."

Payton was surely gratified to hear such words from experts who knew the game from the inside, but he was not the type to bask in his past accomplishments. As early as 1979, he had founded Walter Payton Enterprises; by the time he retired, the firm had a variety of investments, including real estate, timberland, and restaurants. As he turned his attention to running his business, Payton had another ambition in mind: he wanted to be the first African American to own an NFL franchise. After unsuccessfully approaching city officials in Oakland, California, he joined a group of investors hoping to establish a franchise in St. Louis.

Though Payton had never considered money the most important thing in his life, he enjoyed a comfortable life with his family, which now included a son, Jarrett, and a daughter, Brittany. In 1985, Walter and Connie Payton built a spacious 17-room home in the suburbs of Chicago. Walter had taken part in designing the house, which was equipped to accommodate his various hobbies, such as boating, fishing, archery, marksmanship, and his first love—playing the drums. When not at home, he devoted a great deal of time to various charities in the Chicago area, such as the United Way, the March of Dimes, and the Illinois Mental Health Association. Even in retirement, he remained a much-loved figure in Chicago, second in popularity only to the great Cubs shortstop Ernie Banks.

By the 1990s, Payton had tamed his hyperactive nature to the point where he could take his family to Wrigley Field and sit still throughout a baseball game. But he had not lost his love of competition, so he plunged into the world of stock-car racing. When a reporter caught up with him at the track in Lime Rock, Connecticut, in the summer of 1993, the rear end of Payton's Mustang had been demolished in a crash, and he had finished next-to-last in a 22-car field. He was not discouraged. "A lot of the guys I'm racing have been doing this a long time," he said. "I don't care if they take me seriously. . . . If they don't, they'll be behind me."

Two months earlier, Payton had been informed of his election to the Football Hall of Fame. With the induction ceremonies at Canton, Ohio, only a week away, he claimed that he was far more excited about his next auto race. He had been thrilled and honored by the election, but the upcoming ceremony seemed like window dressing to him. Hall of Famers such as Gale Sayers criticized Payton for making such statements, but if Payton had taken the time to congratulate himself, he would not have been the same man who gained 21,736 yards in the NFL.

However, when Payton stood on the dais at the Hall of Fame on July 31, alongside fellow inductees Bill Walsh, Chuck Noll, Larry Little, and Dan Fouts, his attitude changed completely. For one thing, Jarrett Payton, age 12, was at the podium to present his father to the huge crowd assembled in the midsummer sun. Jarrett was the youngest presenter in the history of the Hall of Fame, and he made the most of his opportunity. "Not only is my dad an exceptional athlete," he told the crowd, "he's a role model. He's my biggest role model and best friend. We do a lot of things together—playing basketball, golf, going to movies to name a few. I'm sure my sister will

endorse this statement: we have a super dad."

After wrapping Jarrett in a bear hug, Payton went to the podium and admitted that he had a lump in his throat. He thanked all the people in his life who had, as he said, "taken me under their wings," making special mention of his parents, his high school and college coaches, and

Payton's hunger for speed led him to auto racing after his days of running with the football were over.

former Bears general manager Jim Finks, then suffering from lung cancer. He then confessed that he had not always been an easy man to live with during his 13 NFL seasons and promised to do better. In closing, he told his listeners that "life is short, it's oh so sweet, there are a lot of people we meet as we walk through these hallowed halls, but the things that mean the most are the friendships that you make and take along with you. I'm happy to say that everyone that I've met in my life, I've gained something from them, be it negative or positive, and it has reinforced my life in some aspect."

As a football player and a human being, Walter Payton reinforced many people's lives. Sadly, his own life was taken by cancer on November 1, 1999. Payton was 45 years old.

WALTER PAYTON:
A CHRONOLOGY

1954   Born Walter Jerry Payton in Columbia, Mississippi, on July 25

1968   Joins the football squad at John J. Jefferson High School

1970   Leads Little Dixie Conference in scoring as a high school senior

1971   Enrolls at Jackson State College

1972   Scoring 46 points, including 7 touchdowns, against Lane College, highest total in college football history

1973   Leads nation in scoring with 160 points

1974   Becomes all-time leading scorer in NCAA history with 464 career points

1975   Joins Chicago Bears and runs for 679 yards in rookie season

1976   Marries Connie Norwood; gains 1,390 yards rushing during second season with Bears

1977   Sets NFL single-game rushing mark with 275 yards against Minnesota Vikings; leads NFL with 1,852 yards rushing for the season; becomes the yougest man to be named most valuable player in the NFL

1979   Founds Walter Payton Enterprises

1980   Wins fifth consecutive NFC rushing title

1982   Passes 10,000 yard milestone in rushing

1984   Becomes the NFL's all-time leading rusher

1985   Bears compile a 15-1 regular-season record, en route to triumph in the Super Bowl

1986   Payton passes the 15,000-yard mark in rushing; enjoys 10th 1,000-yard season, an NFL record

1987   Plays 13th and final season with the Bears

1993   Inducted into the Football Hall of Fame

1999   Dies of liver cancer

STATISTICS

WALTER JERRY PAYTON
Chicago Bears

YEAR	RUSHING				PASS RECEIVING			
	ATT	YDS	AVG	TD	CT	YDS	AVG	TD
1975	196	679	3.5	7	39	685	17.6	2
1976	**311**	1390	4.5	**13**	15	149	9.9	0
1977	**339**	**1852**	5.5	**14**	27	269	10.0	2
1978	333	1395	4.2	**11**	50	480	9.6	0
1979	**369**	1610	4.4	**14**	31	313	10.1	2
1980	317	1460	4.6	6	46	367	8.0	1
1981	339	1222	3.6	6	41	379	9.2	2
1982	148	596	4.0	1	32	311	9.7	0
1983	314	1421	4.5	6	53	607	11.5	2
1984	381	1684	4.4	11	45	368	8.2	0
1985	324	1551	4.8	9	49	483	9.9	2
1986	321	1333	4.2	8	37	382	10.3	3
1987	146	533	3.7	4	33	217	6.6	1
TOTALS	**3838**	**16726**	4.4	**110**	498	5010	10.1	17

ATT   attempts
YDS   yards
AVG   average
TD   touchdowns
CT   passes caught

bold indicates league-leading figures

Records still held:
     most rushes, career, 3838
     most rushing yardage, career, 16726
     most rushing TDs, career, 110
     most combined yardage (rushing and receiving), career, 21736
     most 1000-yard rushing seasons, 10
     most 100-yard games, career, 77

SUGGESTIONS FOR FURTHER READING

Lamb, Kevin. *Portrait of Victory: Chicago Bears 1985.* (A National Football League Book.) Chicago: Bonus Books, 1986.

Madden, John, and Dave Anderson. *One Knee Equals Two Feet (& Everything Else You Need To Know About Pro Football).* New York: Villard Books, 1986.

Payton, Walter, with Jerry B. Jenkins. *Sweetness.* Chicago: Contemporary Books, 1978.

Pierson, Don, and Jonathan Daniel. *The Super Season.* Chicago: Bonus Books, 1986.

Whittingham, Richard. *Bears in Their Own Words.* Chicago: Contemporary Books, 1991.

———. *The Chicago Bears: An Illustrated History.* Revised ed. New York: Simon & Schuster, 1986.

ABOUT THE AUTHOR

Philip Koslow is a New York-based writer and editor who grew up rooting for the Giants and still believes they would have beaten the Bears in the 1963 championship game if Y. A. Tittle had not been injured. The editor of numerous books for young readers, he is also the author of *El Cid* in the Chelsea House HISPANICS OF ACHIEVEMENT series and of *The Seminole Indians* in Chelsea House's JUNIOR LIBRARY OF AMERICAN INDIANS.

INDEX